RENEWAL
POETRY

PRAISE FOR HARRY'S POETRY

"Harry, your spiritual journey is apparent from the richness of your poetry.... For reminding me of some of the light that has shown through the darkness and grays of my own life's journey, I gratefully thank you. Congratulations.... As a scientist and writer of prose I know little of the syntax of poetry, but enough to appreciate the saying that while prose speaks to the mind, poetry speaks to the heart. It would be a cold stone heart that would not warm and beat the stronger for having read Harry Azmitia's poetry."

— Dr. Ronald M. DiSalvo, CSci, CChem, FRSC. Member of the Royal Institution of Great Britain, The Association of Formulating Chemists, The American Academy of Science, The New York Academy of Science, and The American Academy of Anti-Aging Medicine.

"As I read your poems Harry I am struck with your depth and sensitivity. They are moving and stir the heart...."

— Ellen Tadd: Clairvoyant, Counselor, Lecturer, Instructor.

"Edmund Rostand's wonderful character and warrior poet Cyrano DeBergerac, once decried poetry as a game of words. Harry Azmitia's 21 poems are no game but linguistic monuments to the very essence of life and to humankind's massive and often hidden struggles to stay spiritually, emotionally, physically and mentally alive. As a veteran of the Vietnam War, Harry knows about the struggle to stay alive. Warriors of all kinds know this struggle better than us all. Warriors know the abrupt ending that is death; one minute alive and the next, not. Warriors know the crises of each new beginning that follows each new end; of each breath's choices made and of prices paid. In each of his poems this tilting balance and the love he reaches for time and again is the renewal of his life and of each of our lives in turn."

— Cheryl Howland, M.Ed., C.A.G.S.,
Assistant Director/Academic Access Services,
Disability Services Office, University of
Massachusetts, Amherst.

PREFACE

Through my voice and reflections, I want my poetry to illuminate feelings and desires that stir the heart, soul, and spirit. My poems explore the awakening of wonder, the mystery of love and life, and the courage to live with spiritual values. Within my poetry, there are glimpses of my personal life, spiritual journey, and wisdom to live an authentic life. I invite the reader to contemplate the significance of these messages in their own lives.

RENEWAL
POETRY

HARRY NORMAN AZMITIA, JR.

Copyright © 2012 Harry Norman Azmitia, Jr.

All rights reserved. No part of this book may be used or reproduced or transmitted in any form or by any means, electronic or mechanical, including photocopying, recording, or by any information storage and retrieval system, without written permission of the publisher except where permitted by law.

For information contact Harry Norman Azmitia, Jr. at P. O. Box 60356, Florence, MA 01062 or at h3a9jr@gmail.com.

Printed in the United States of America

ISBN:978-0-9885927-2-8

Booksmyth Press
Shelburne Falls, MA 01370
www.thebooksmyth.com

In Loving Memory

~

Magdelena Azmitia

Edwin Rios

Rene Carbajal Azmitia

Helen Frankovitz Toiber Dubow

Jack and Gary Dubow

Harry and Hencha Frankovitz

Vincent Ragone

Beatrice Stealman

Contents

Trust	1
Lost	3
Spring	5
Fall	7
The Gift	8
You	9
To See	10
Your Rose	11
Love's Clarity	12
My Mother	13
A Song To Remember	15
Tears	16
My Cat	17
Sage	19
Twenty-Fifth Anniversary	21
Barack Obama's Inauguration	23
Unsung Heroes	25
Bewildered	29
The Reluctant Cupid	31
The Awakening	33
Divine Wheel	36
Biography	41
Acknowledgments	43
Note on Sources	45

POEMS

Through my voice and reflections, I want my poetry to illuminate feelings and desires that stir the heart, soul, and spirit. My poems explore the awakening of wonder, the mystery of love and life, and the courage to live with spiritual values. Within my poetry, there are glimpses of my personal life, spiritual journey, and wisdom to live an authentic life. I invite the reader to contemplate the significance of these messages in their own lives.

Trust

Huge problems are brought to bear
    As one copes with life,
Solutions are neither here nor there
    While one is in deep strife,
In considering a problem's scale
    Under its turbulent weight,
Think of this mariner's tale
    And of his appointed fate.

The ship sailed on a calm sea
    With the sky and world in order,
When a dark cloud loomed with a swift breeze
    A storm brewed at horizon's border,
Caught in the storm
    Howling winds persist,
As darkness formed
    On a course amiss,
As the ship was bound
    With high tides,
Waves came crashing down
    On the ship's sides,
While on downward and upward slopes
    The ship swayed back and forth,
The men cried out for faith and hope
    Salvation from south or north,
Calling on their inner source
    Their manner was transformed,
With hands in prayer to a mighty force
    For a miracle to form ;

The sea turned calmer than before
    With gentle waves far and wide,
As the ship sailed towards a peaceful shore
    The sun shined through a brilliant sky.

Let this tale take hold
    To those who will listen,
One may think they're in control
    In a life that glistens,
But when a problem is revealed
    In its massive scale,
It is wise to yield
    In order to prevail.

Lost

Holding a lifeless body,
What story to refer?
Not just anybody;
I'm awfully sorry sir.

In a land so far,
And involved in war,
With a body scarred,
In God I implore.

Adjusting his bloody collar
It seems surreal,
Holding his hand, holding my holler,
With thoughts remorseful and ideal.

He was brave and bold,
As I try to hold
My sanity no more,
With a rage a glow
I run and roar!

Experiencing great pain
And death so wasteful,
Feeling disgust, great shame,
And disgraceful.

Holding tender hand, tender sir,
The question will never end,
What glory to refer?
Many thoughts to mend
And to send,
For we will never part,
He will always live
In my mind and in my heart.

Prayer to thee
Almighty Lord,
On bended knee
I implore,
Take his soul
So brave and bold,
And with your guiding wisdom,
Talk to him, walk with him,
To your mighty kingdom.

Spring

The land is wet from melting snow
    Which winter held so dear,
Spring waits for her face to show
    In air so fresh and clear.

Walking beside a babbling stream
    In perfect harmony,
Colors appear I've never seen
    In dream or memory.

Looking up at an old oak tree
    Where leaves are fresh and new,
Eager Robin prepares to feed
    Her tiny and hungry brood.

Birds perch to spread their wings
    High above the tree,
Brace to fly and begin to sing
    In pitched and joyful glee.

Spring consumes this holy place!
    Leaving behind the cold and dark,
Fair spring in graceful haste
    Renews and leaves her mark.

Give praise to nature's ways
    And God's mighty hand,
To joyful times and joyful days
    As spring spreads throughout the land.

Fall

Summer filled with flowers
   In full bloom,
I could sit for hours
   Breathing sweet perfume.

Summer can be traced
   By the glowing sun,
In this majestic space
   Of warm horizons.

Fall arrives
   With colorful leaves,
Cherished scenes revive
   When memories are weaved.

Frost on the lawn
   Sure signs of winter,
Just behind the dawn
   Gray skies will enter.

Winter white with snow
   Crowned with Christmas day,
Hands in prayer to show
   Gratitude and praise.

From where I sit
   I see summer and winter,
Translucent climates within sunlit
   And moonlit centers.

The Gift

You read me poetry,
    Words with colorful emotions,
Like God's creation of the earth and sea,
    Expressions of love and devotions.

You brought me flowers,
    A sign of affection,
With each petal I count the hours,
    Filled with every recollection.

You brought me diamonds,
    To light my way,
Glittering islands,
    On a sunlit bay.

Greatest gift of all,
    You brought yourself to me,
Thoughts I still recall,
    Memories of you and me.

You

Your radiant face
    Makes me shine,
With a wisdom
    That's divine,
When my mood lies in
    The deepest blue,
Your knowing smile makes me
    See what's true,
When there doesn't seem
    To be any hope,
And my life is on
    A downward slope,
You enter with
    A point of view,
Giving hope to what's
    Divinely true,
Hope for the best
    On any given time,
For darkness leaves
    When there's true sunshine,
Hope for the best
    On the side of God,
Say yes to life
    With the slightest nod;
Your sweet face
    Makes me want for more,
For the many charms
    I do adore.

To See

To see a flower
    Blooming with the sun,
One is empowered
    By beauty begun.

To see a sunrise
    Each day renewed,
Brilliance to eyes
    Majestic gold and blue.

To see a sunset
    It's beauty alone,
Inspiration is met
    When colored skies roam.

To see a new born
    Holding its toes,
Stretching to yawn
    Time for sleep it knows.

To see kindness unfold
    With each passing day,
A sight to behold
    There's no other way.

To see those blessed
    With wrong ways undone,
Could truly impress
    The God in each one.

Your Rose

Among the flowers stands a white rose
    Its green leaves shaped like spears,
With a sweet aroma so composed
    Which permeates the atmosphere.

Will it be plucked
    For a glorious scene?
Or will it be plucked
    For some want or dream?

Is it for a sad event
    Being laid on a coffin for a life spent,
Might it be for festive fare
    To be held at a wedding then thrown in the air,
Or will it be tossed at sea
    For a loved one with a final plea.

Perhaps it should be left alone,
    To its beauty and majestic tone,
The white rose symbol of purity,
    A gift from God, a true gift for thee.

Love's Clarity

I pray for divine power
    To understand life's fire,
And to know each waking hour
    May be joyful and inspired.

One word universally spoken
    And this word is love,
When taken as a token
    Has the white purity of a dove.

Love in all its glory
    Is to be shared with all people,
To joyfully hear loving stories
    And wedding bells from steeples.

Love is like a song
    That fills one's mind with clarity,
With a meaning that is strong
    And with a wondrous melody.

Love offers strength indeed
    Messages of hope and grace,
For those with the greatest need
    Love fills an empty space.

Love surpasses even death
    And is brilliant as a dawn,
With love in ones last breath
    Life continues on.

My Mother

Here lays my mother
   In this holy shrine,
While overwhelmed with grief and disbelief,
   Wondering and pondering to the divine,
I pray and cry
   "There will be no other."

Solemnly I come to this holy place
   Wanting to hold and caress,
With hands in prayer I silently confess
   For God's full embrace,
Though tears and words were
   Never spoken,
I cry out and fall heartbroken.

At my mother's grave
   While sobbing and weeping,
Forgetful thoughts emerge
   Which are sweeping,
Remembering her glad at plain
   And honest gain,
Recalling her sad and strain
   Through life's pain,
Remembering more than I can bare
   Even more heartbroken,
Thoughts emerged that pierced the dark
   Thoughts that were hardly spoken,
When mother passed beyond the reality veil,
   The angels gathered and hailed,

"God will embrace and hold
   And take care of this heavenly soul,"
While grasping this comforting thought,
   Another memory not distraught
Emerged like the sun's glow
   Wide and bold,
I must say on her behalf,
   "She had a radiant laugh."

From all the scenes that are recalled
   These are the cherished ones overall,
Remembering mother healing my hurts
   With a gentle word or touch,
Recalling her protecting me
   From the world
I felt safe and secure
   For she loved me so much,
With outstretched arms to Heaven above,
   One defining prayer is hurled,
"Seeing and feeling our great love
   For each other,
Dear God, I would give anything
   To have once more my mother."

A Song To Remember

Be not gloomy on the morrow,
Steeped in grief and heavy sorrow,
In her passing she left us cheer,
Abundant memories from there to here,
Her grace was borne on tender wings,
For God, friendship and offspring,
Like birdsong raised in exquisite note,
Her voice lingers in glory and hope,
Her smile still sparkles in radiant light,
Though she's been taken to heaven's height,
Her life was full and fine and true,
A timeless melody for me and you.

Tears

In life one sheds tears at one time or another,
For reasons far or near or for reasons undiscovered.

A memory with an emotional hold,
In tearful reverie of a magical place of old.

Tears displayed at weddings joyful events indeed,
Couples forward headings blessed by Gods' decree.

Dealing with death and dying extremely hard to bear,
Grieving alone is sad if one isn't willing to share.

Tears gone, one might see through worldly veils,
A different world indeed as the Bible tells.

My Cat

Lucky's fur makes me laugh
He's wearing a tuxedo with white gloves,
His profile is class
And he's one of my greatest loves.

Sitting by the front door
His lantern eyes tells me he wants to explore,
I open the door and he rises from the floor,
Walking outside the world offers more.

His movements are graceful as a swan,
Walking beside him
I realize it is dawn,
For the evening is luminous and dim.

Lucky's nostrils open and close
Rising and falling like waves along shores,
I think he knows
That tempting smells are only lures.

Sitting with content
One paw on top of the other,
A time well spent,
I fancy conversing with one another.

Several experiences I assert,
He listens and takes it all in,
Telling my dream, desire and hurt,
I imagine him knowing where I've been.

I ask did he want to go home,
He looked at me then turned around,
Walking with body full grown
Smelling the air and ground.

When too tired to walk
I hold him like an only son,
Tenderly kissing with quieting talk
For he is the only one.

The door is open
I stroke his black and white fur,
Thanking him often
He answers with a deep purr.

With Lucky I'm never alone
For he gives me pleasure and joy,
My voice has a loving tone
Each time I observe his playful ploy.

We are well suited
Our trust cannot be broken,
Like a tree firmly rooted
Nourishment is love that's not spoken.

I love my Lucky, my cat, my friend,
Like the peace symbol of a dove,
When bad moods start to set in,
They are replaced with Lucky's love.

SAGE

Moans and groans from the other room
    My wife and I could clearly hear,
Giving support as we assumed
    A new life would soon be here.

We entered the room
    Where three midwives stood,
Caring from morning till noon
    Our daughter into motherhood.

While each midwife took her place
    A tub was filled with water,
Inside with water line to waist
    Sat the expectant daughter.

Great care was focused on her
    Breathing heavy and ready to deliver,
Time for the miracle to occur
    To give life and be a true giver.

Suddenly the baby came out
    From beneath the water line,
As I imagined God giving a great shout
    It's life at its prime!

Baby was lifted above the water,
    As the twisted cord was cut from her skin,
There sat with beading sweat an exhausted daughter,
    Beside herself with a grin.

The midwives did their duty,
    Like a plump cherub with red cheeks
And radiant beauty,
    The baby's health was at its peak.

My wife and I with gaiety
    Saw this miracle unfold,
Like being in sublimity
    Reality was hard to uphold.

As midwives gave victory nods
    To one another,
Like a gift from a majestic God
    Sage was handed to her grateful mother.

Twenty-Fifth Anniversary

This is a special day
   A day to celebrate,
For the love displayed
   On a daily rate.

Today is an anniversary
   In its golden state,
Success through adversities
   We needn't calibrate.

In the beginning
   Unsure of our trust,
We found ourselves grinning
   Insecurities didn't bother us.

Surprise unveiled upon
   The time explored,
Wrong expectations gone
   Found we wanted more.

We noticed strong bonds
   Without words ever spoken,
Like pebbles thrown in ponds
   Loving waves felt often.

In each other's company
   Love was expressed,
With joy and harmony
   We were at our best.

When problems did occur
   We became involved,
No matter what they were
   Together we did solve.

Mistakes we did accept
   Like diamonds with flaws,
Precious to be kept
   Without perfect cores.

Faith in love and hope
   Our love will grow and last,
Like horizon's scope
   Our future seems so vast.

So raise your silver cup
   And give a hearty toast,
Seeing us close up
   It's true love at its most.

Barack Obama's Inauguration

You restored faith and hope
   In the United States,
Looking at horizon's scope
   America strong and great.

With action and eloquent talk
   You restored honor and pride,
Like a white dove and a dark hawk
   America's strength is side by side.

We pray for success
   In your privileged position,
A leader who's blessed
   Gets results despite opposition.

You understand and are on guard
   Of America's friends and foes,
Decisions will be very hard
   As your term in office grows.

By electing you Commander in Chief
   A White House resident,
You have demonstrated the belief
   Any child can grow to be President.

Americans will celebrate
   This historic inauguration,
Those who choose not to partake
   Are accepted in this great nation.

Given America's economic distress
    And the worlds' dramas,
Solutions will be wisely addressed
    When hope is restored by President Obama.

Unsung Heroes

When walking thru the park
   I would often think,
What initiates the heroic spark?
   Hopeful to receive a hint.

With each step slowly
   Being taken,
Like a pilgrim seeking the wise and holy,
   Thoughts of heroism were awaken.

An eerie silence after the thick of combat,
   Like being on the edge of a fence,
In foxholes Marines sat,
   Counting their ordinance.

With the action down
   Marines helping each other,
Faces with dark frowns
   Counting the dead true brothers.

Then near their rim
   A thumping sound,
A grenade for them
   On the hard ground.

A Marine fell
   On the grenade,
No time to yell
   He did it for the friends he made.

A Fireman
    Runs into a structure that burns,
He time and time again
    Saves lives without personal concern.

Out of the bellowing smoke
    In a terrible rush,
To an ambulance as he choked,
    Holding something small and flush.

He with agitation
    With a baby draped over his arm,
Giving mouth to mouth resuscitation
    Trying to save this young charm.

Finally he couldn't deny
    Hope was truly gone,
While holding the baby he cried
    Realizing life without its bond.

Others assured him
    He did all he could,
Words interim
    With thoughts of the greater good.

Single mother with children to protect and care
    Actions without restraint,
Like a cape of burdens too great to bare
    She wore without complaint.

Two lionesses on the hunt
    Gazelles to be ambushed,
One walking in front
    While the other sat in the bush.

For some strange reason
    A lioness had a change of heart,
Though it was hunting season
    She succumbed to a mysterious part.

She took a fawn
    As her own,
Like caring for a newborn
    She gently licked the fawn's cheekbone.

A female dog
    Giving milk to kittens,
At play a mystery dialogue
    That cannot be written.

While walking near a brook
    Heard a distant noise,
I turned to look
    As I kept my poise.

Sounds fading in and out
    From a big oak tree,
There without a doubt
    Robins a group of three.

Two baby Robins nearly twice the size
    As their frail mother,
She tries to rise
    To feed open mouths as they fluttered.

Heroic scenes which are brave and true
    Images with mystery in mind,
Like an orchestra conductor giving cues
    God answers at the right time.

Bewildered

To have an unjust act
    Caused by a lover,
Like a stabbing in the heart,
    Mindful still, I cannot recover.

To lose my love
    In an untimely death,
Like a soaring dove,
    Until her last breath.

To feel another's pain,
    My heart grows tired and weak,
Like young innocence slain,
    Mother's eyes, wet and bleak.

One without hurt
    Is what I seek,
Like Hercules shouldering the world,
    He cannot divert,
Given his strength at its peak.

To take my life
    And be no more,
Like a dead soldier away from strife
    Away from war.

To dream, to think, to feel,
    As one who is alive,
Like a monk who kneels
    And prays towards the heavenly side.

To dream the dream
    Of world peace,
With Cupid as a theme
    Effecting hate to cease.

Almighty God I implore,
    A prayer while on bended knee,
To be, or
    Not to be?

The Reluctant Cupid

Cupid outside my heart,
Don't turn and depart,
Leaving me alone
By having my life end
    With Never Truly Loved on a gravestone.

Empty is life and empty I cope
Having little faith and hope;
Cupid freeing me from the dark
Will leave your mark
As God's faithful envoy,
So don't deny me the greatest of joy,
To love all things and beings not from afar,
To be embraced by almighty God.

Cupid clear away my fright
And chase the night,
By ridding me of my plight
To receive God's light,
So aim your arrow
And strike at my heart at its narrow.

Cupid you've granted my request
God bless you and god bless the rest,
For when I was blind as night
You let love shine forth into a brilliant sight,
By aiming and shooting at this poor soul
And striking my heart to make me whole,
You've guided me to see and to be,
To love me and the we,

To love from the beginning to the end,
To live and to give now and then again,
To be filled with joy that surpasses understanding,
To have a love that's constantly expanding,
To be one with God
And not from afar,
To be in the now with God and I as one,
And to share this precious love, this precious joy,
    Until my time is done.

The Awakening

In my agnostic past
   Studied spiritual books,
Like dark and light which contrast,
    Knowledge gave new outlooks.

Searching for my Spirit center
   Meditated for solutions,
As darkness leaves and sunrise enters,
    Enlightened by resolutions.

Psychic gifts ahead
   At the right time,
Like walking a mystery road which led,
    To awareness and the sublime.

Having found grace and peace
   Like two white feathers floating on air,
Many worries and problems ceased
    While holding the fleeting pair.

My world in a peaceful state,
   Helping people in life,
Although peace was on any date,
    Life gave too much strife.

Psychic gifts were lost,
   While struggling for many years,
Forgotten abilities at great cost,
    Life filled with doubts and fears.

Then one night in a dream
    An angelic being took the lead,
Three Archangels seem to gleam
    Messengers they seemed to be.

Archangels to make senses right
    To unclog and to forge them bright,
Psychic healing and sight
    Returned to me that night.

Along with psychic gifts,
    Received guidance and wisdom,
Guiding those who would be adrift
    With help from the messenger threesome.

With sun light warming my face
    Awakened with joy and peace,
Like a golden shrine in a holy place
    Wanting these feelings to never cease.

My life with a difference
    Is filled with faith and hope,
Using my dream as reference
    Whenever problems are too much to cope.

People who are drawn to me
    Seeking answers and signs,
Failing to see they're the key
    To their problems at any time.

Looking here and beyond,
    The past and tomorrows,
Praying I wisely respond
    To life's joys and sorrows.

Divine Wheel

From a Spirit
   Emanates a Soul,
A spark of fire growing and glowing
   Into an eternal burn,
Too much for eyes
   To see and behold,
To settle past life traumas
   Soul seeks lessons to learn.

Soul incarnates
   Into an innocent infant,
Like sculptured statues
   With excellence and perfections,
Growing with relations
   Difficult and different,
At times success
   After trials and tribulations.

The person is given life
   As well as a will,
To choose
   What is right or wrong,
Like traveling rough terrains
   Up and down hills,
Reaching summits
   The Spirit sings a song.

If the person grows
   To become materialistic,
Like having many items
   When there's too much to owe,
Faith in abundant things
   Is unrealistic,
The Spirit awaits
   For the person to know.

If the person decides
   To strive for great power,
Because Godlike feelings
   Are alluring,
Like time itself
   There's a finite hour,
Spirit is hopeful
   Person's aware it's not enduring.

If the person leads an unhappy life
   The Spirit hopes
For the person to embrace
   The light within,
Like a blind man in darkness
   Having to grope,
The person seeks joy
   And the time to begin.

The person in awe
  Of a majestic sunrise,
Like seeing a huge ball
  Emitting golden light,
Instantly the person
  Comes to recognize,
The answer
  To its joyless plight.

Whatever life offers
  The person meditates,
Like monks resonating chants
  To the above,
With each meditation
  The person gravitates,
Towards compassion
  And love.

The person's life ends
  Soul returns to Spirit,
Like a glistening rain drop falling into
  An expansive blue ocean,
One with Infinite Spirit
  With True Love within it,
Infinite Spirit is all
  And deserves devotion.

BIOGRAPHY

Harry Norman Azmitia, Jr. was born on December 20, 1949. He grew up in a poor, integrated neighborhood in New York City. At age thirteen, his father abandoned him and left his mother with four children to support. At fifteen, Harry dropped-out of Junior High School and stayed away from friends because they were using illegal drugs. He kept to himself and studied Art and Astronomy.

At seventeen, he worked as a Merchant Marine and sailed on a ship. At eighteen, Harry joined the United States Marine Corps for four years and was well trained as an infantryman. In 1969 at the height of the Vietnam War, he was in South Vietnam and assigned to Bravo Company, 1st Battalion, 9th Marine Regiment, 3rd Marine Division, also known as "1/9 The Walking Dead." His Company and Battalion patrolled South of the Demilitarized Zone in the Quang Tri province. After Vietnam, he received a General Education Diploma.

After four years in the Marine Corps, Harry continued his education by first attending a Junior College then a four year Private College. He could not make ends meet with the G.I. Bill, so he worked at the colleges as an Evening Building Maintenance Worker, so he could attend day classes. It took Harry fourteen years to obtain a Bachelor of Science in Computer Science, and he later went on to receive a Professional Certificate in Micro Computer Engineering. He worked for companies that dealt with computer programming, but found he was not a corporate person.

When Harry was laid-off from a computer job in 2002, it gave him the opportunity to address his problems relating to Vietnam. He sought advice from a counselor at the Vet Center in Springfield, Massachusetts. He found that he had combat Post Traumatic Stress Disorder. After several consultations, Harry entered the Post Traumatic Stress Disorder program in Ward 8 at the VA Medical Center (Veterans Hospital) in Northampton, Massachusetts. While at Ward 8 in 2004, for the first time in his life he wrote a poem "Lost," about an experience in Vietnam. Since then, he has written twenty inspired poems on different subjects.

Harry believed the way out of poverty was to get a college education in order to succeed. This is true, but he feels and knows there is more to life.

He will continue to be inspired by people and nature. Life is not only about the material, it is about creativity, love, and God.

Harry continues to write poems to stir the heart, soul, and spirit.

ACKNOWLEDGMENTS

I am grateful to my wife, Sandra D. Azmitia, for her help and unfailing support throughout my struggle with combat Post Traumatic Stress Disorder (PTSD). Although each of us has their own journey in life, we are companions in one voyage. She enabled me to write inspired poems.

To my spouse's daughter Lisa Zimmerman who suspected I had PTSD due to my experiences in the Vietnam War, I am thankful for her advice which led me to seek help at the Vet Center in Springfield, Massachusetts.

To Ellen Tadd, I appreciate her and her inspired lectures, instructions, and clairvoyant consultations. But most of all, I appreciate the spiritual gifts that she offers to humanity and nature.

Special thanks to Dr. Ronald M. DiSalvo, although a scientist he is a poet at heart, and to Cheryl Howland who has helped many students with disabilities at the University of Massachusetts, Amherst.

I also acknowledge the Veterans Center's counselors who have helped and supported me with my combat PTSD; namely, David Bressam, Dianne M. Hilgreth, and Dr. Merredith S. McCarran.

Although not associated with the Veterans Center, I have received counsel from Dr. Peggy Perri, a former combat nurse during the Vietnam War.

To the staff at Ward 8 of the VA Medical Center (VAMC) in Northampton, Massachusetts: Dr. Richard Pearlstein (who has helped veterans, especially combat veterans) and Dr. Greg Firman; Physician Assistant Bruce Bennett; Intake Coordinator Wayne Lynch; Ward Clerk Dolores Elliott; Social Workers John

Christopher, Sherrill Ashton; Nurses Fran Lunny, Judy Zahn, Frank Bertrand, Dwight Kelley, Brooks Ryder, Joe Polito; Mental Health Associates Mike Connor, Alex Provost; Nutritionist Barbara Graf; Priest Lionel Bonneville; and to the staff at the main building, Dr. Mir H. Hashimi, Dr. Howard D. Klein, Social Worker Lillian R. Struckus. I am extremely grateful for all their help and support with my combat PTSD.

Outside the VAMC, my sincere thanks to Dr. Michael R. Verrilli, Dr. Emily Clionsky, Dr. Marc Goldman, LPN Julie Rehm, all of whom have compassion and care for their patients. To the founders of The Florence Poets Society, Carl Russo and Thomas Clark, who gave me the encouragement and space to express my poetry. My thanks also to Maureen Moore's Literary Salon and for her help and support in publishing this book.

NOTE ON SOURCES

Book cover image of the star LL Pegasi, from ESA/NASA & R. Sahai

Ellen Tadd: Clairvoyant, Counselor, Lecturer, Instructor. www.ellentadd.com

This book was composed, with pleasure,
using Minion Pro digital typeface

www.ingramcontent.com/pod-product-compliance
Lightning Source LLC
LaVergne TN
LVHW051202080426
835508LV00021B/2768